A SEA OF DRIFTWOOD

Photographs by Elizabeth Kramer

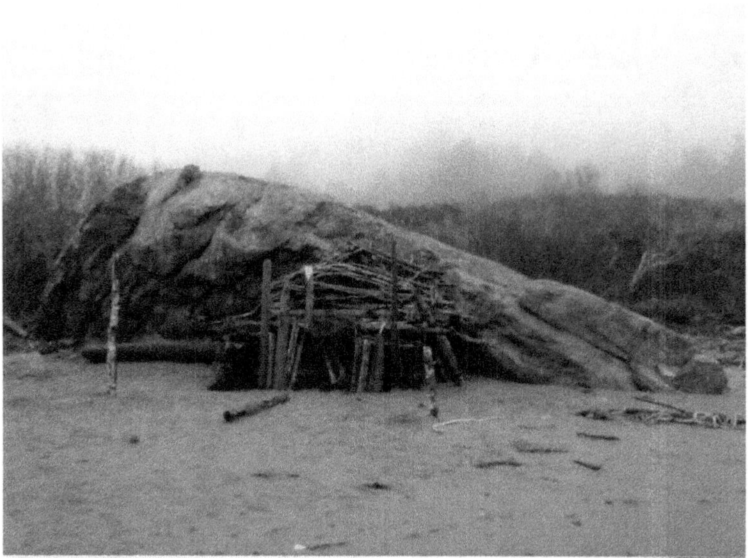

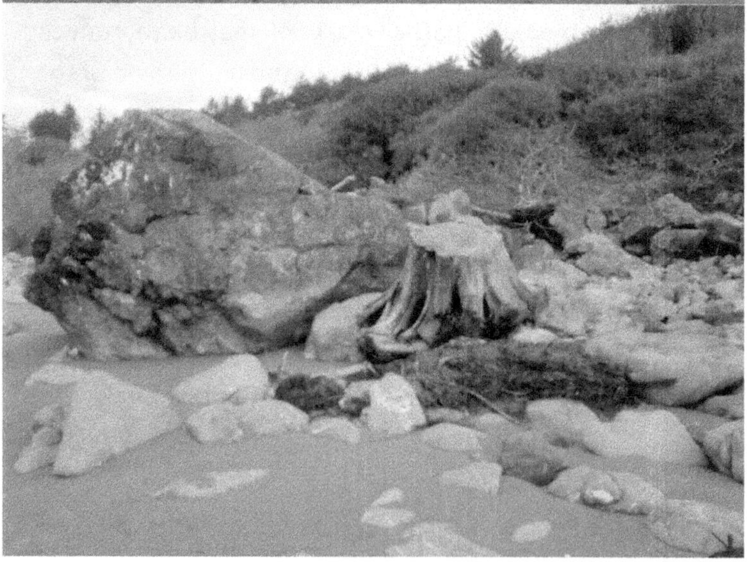

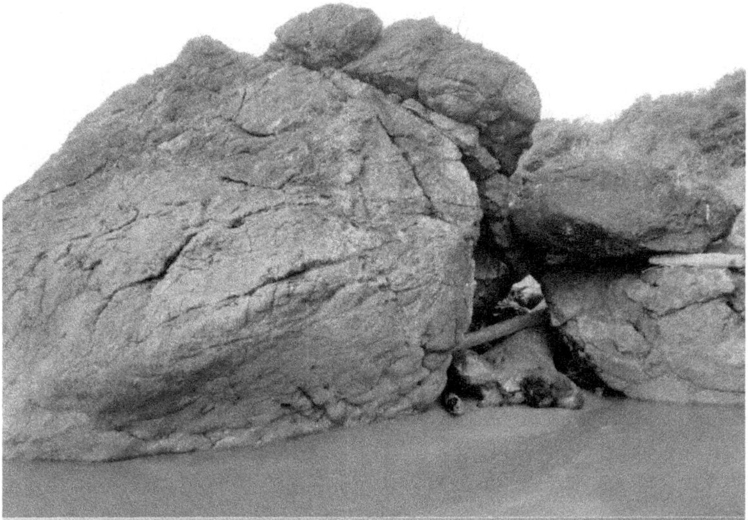

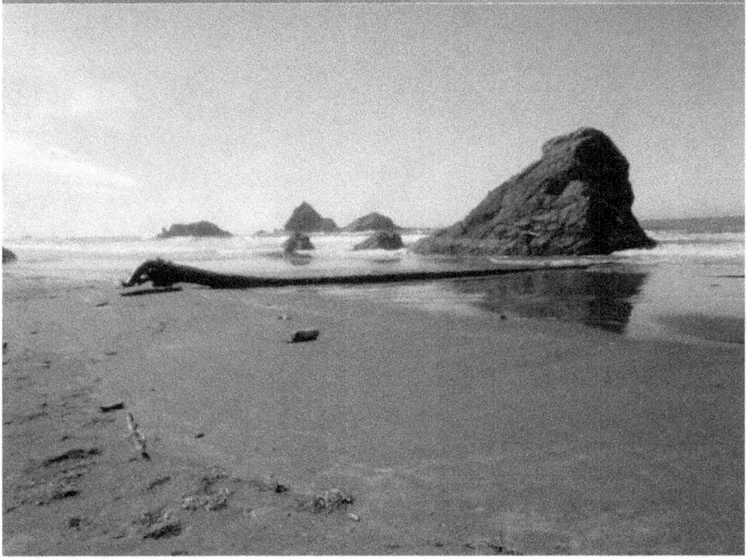

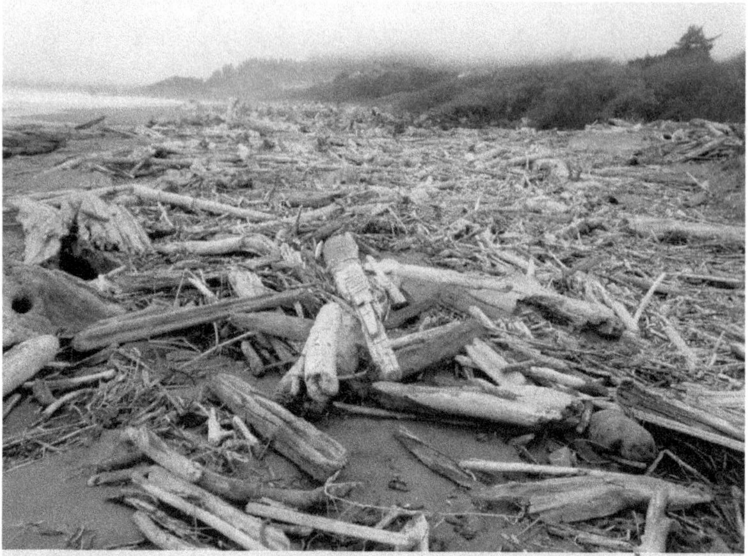
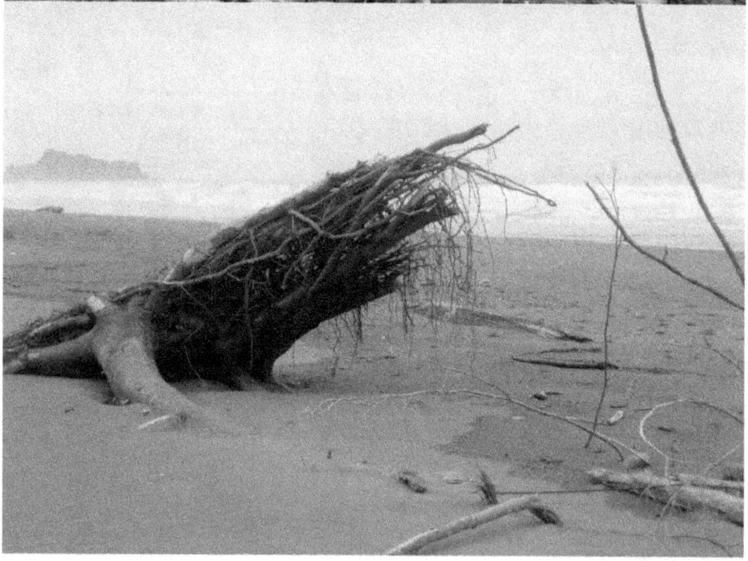

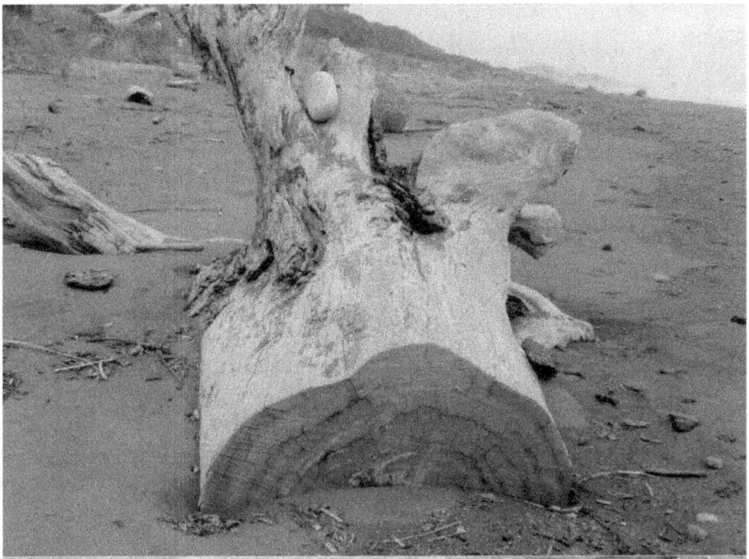
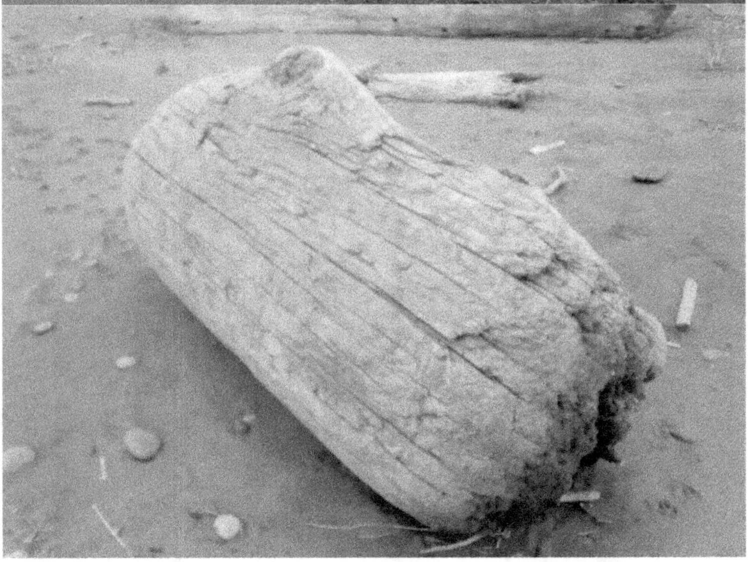

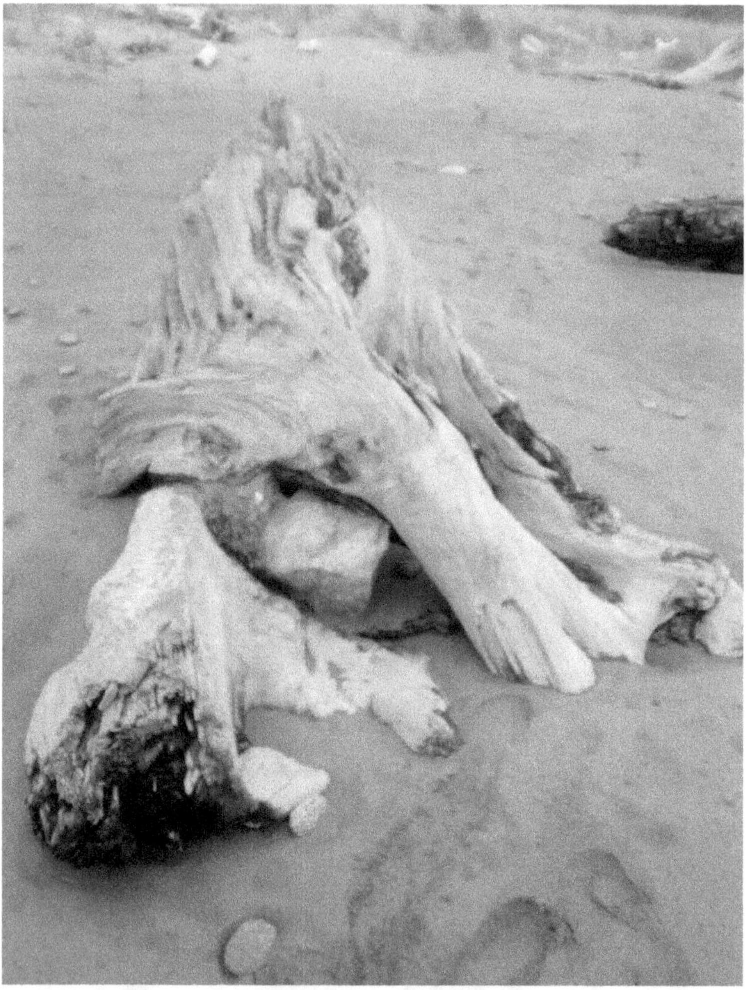

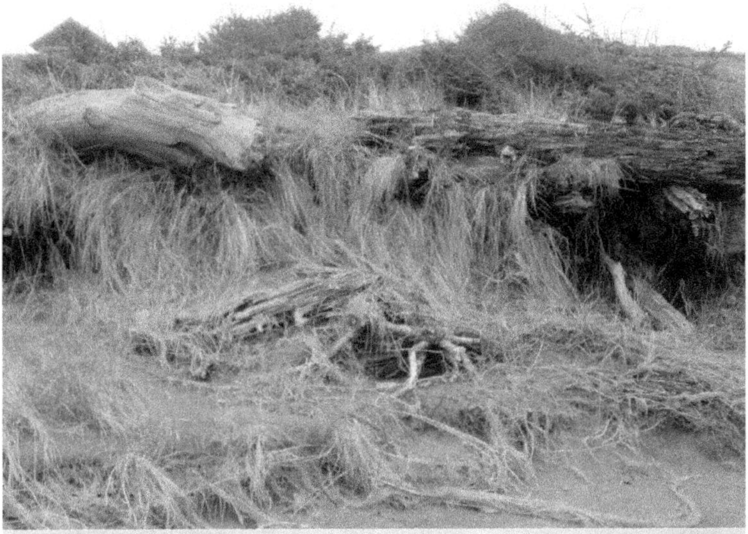

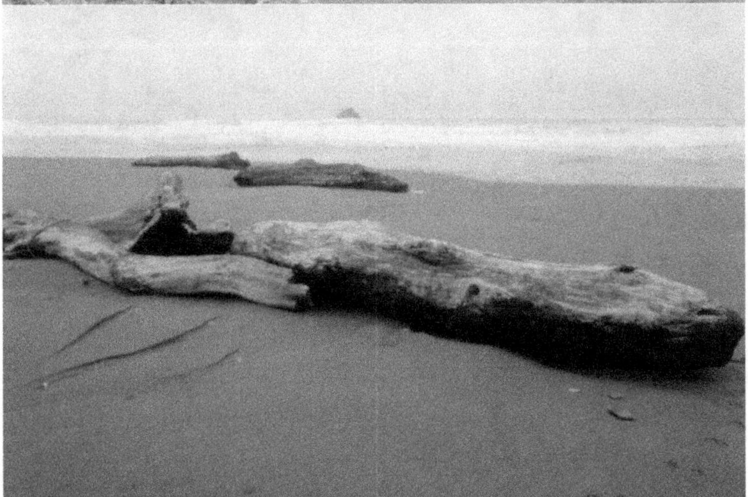

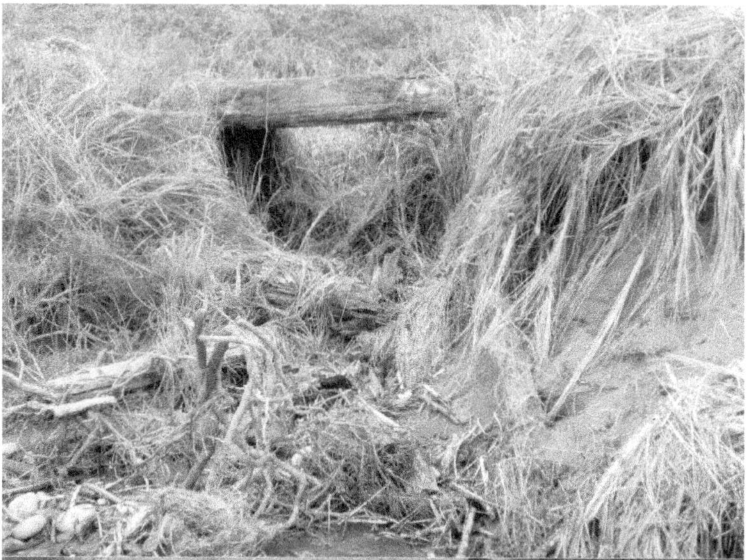

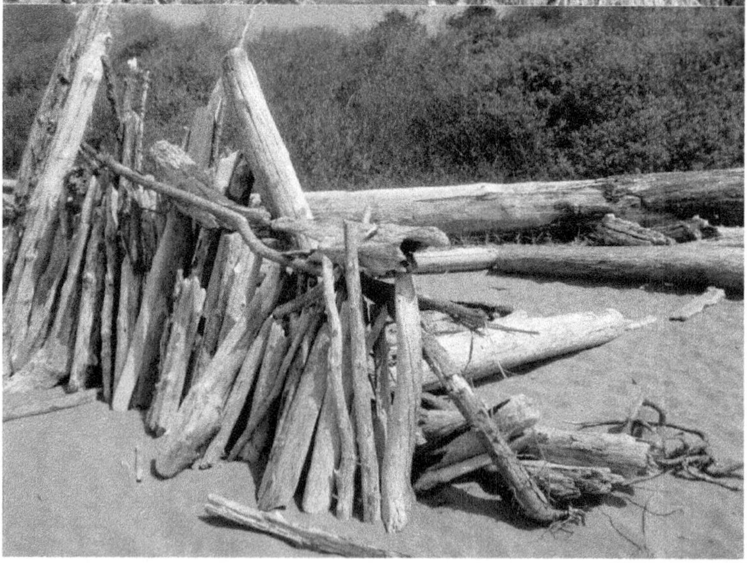

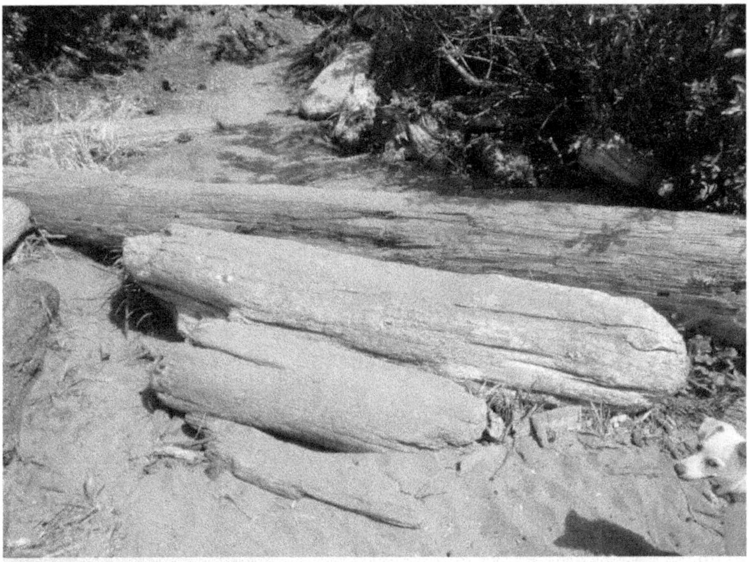

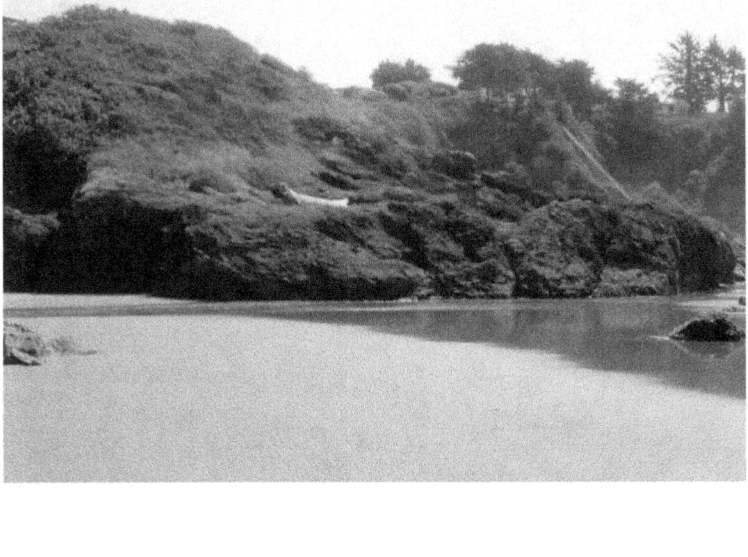

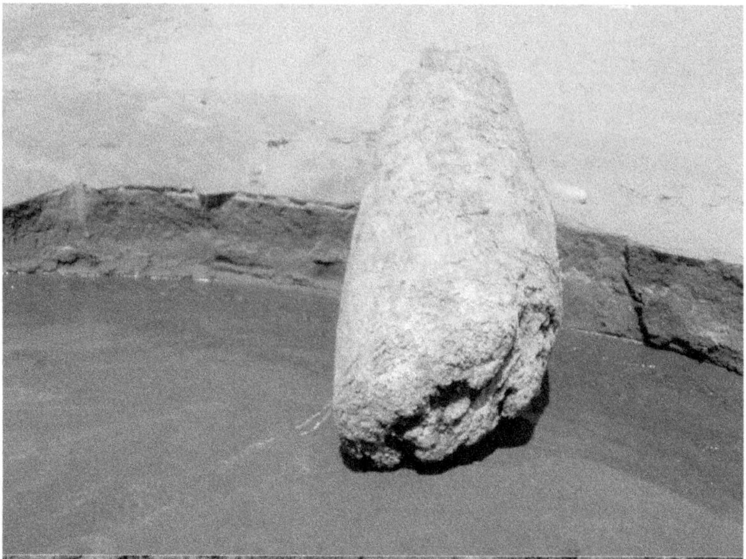

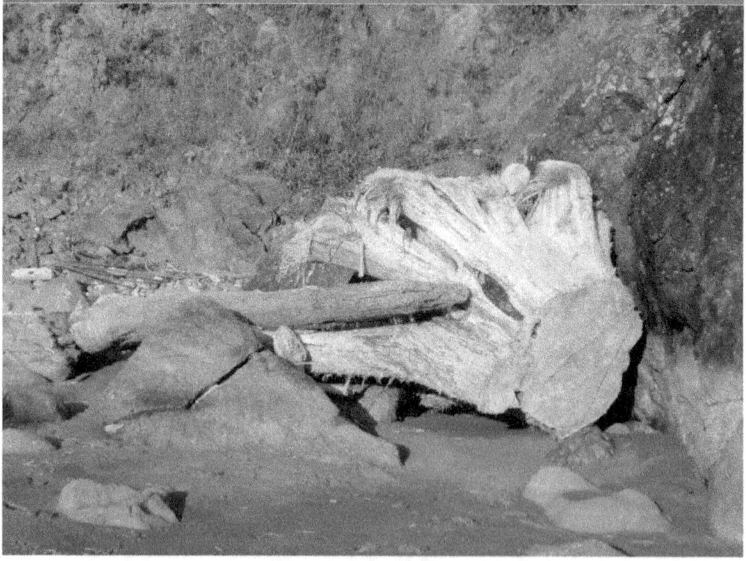

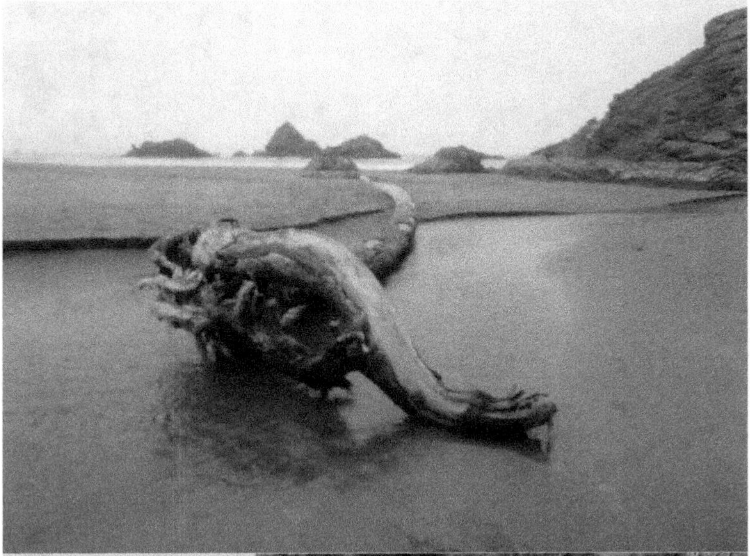

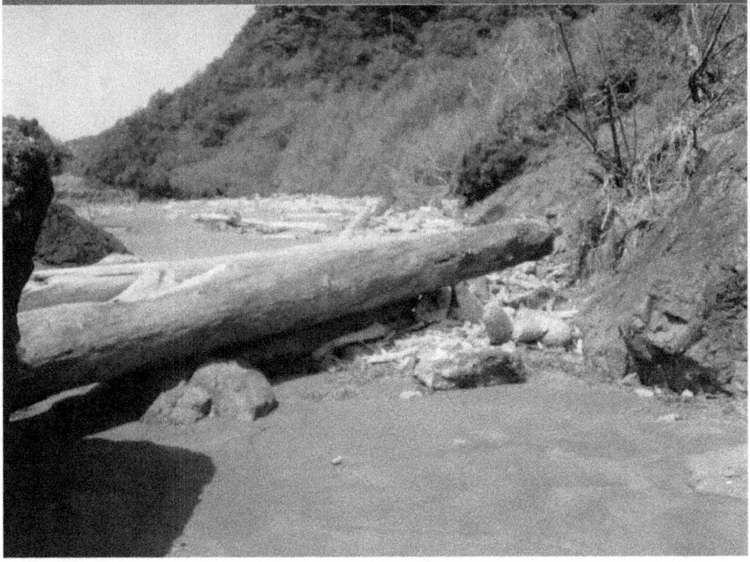

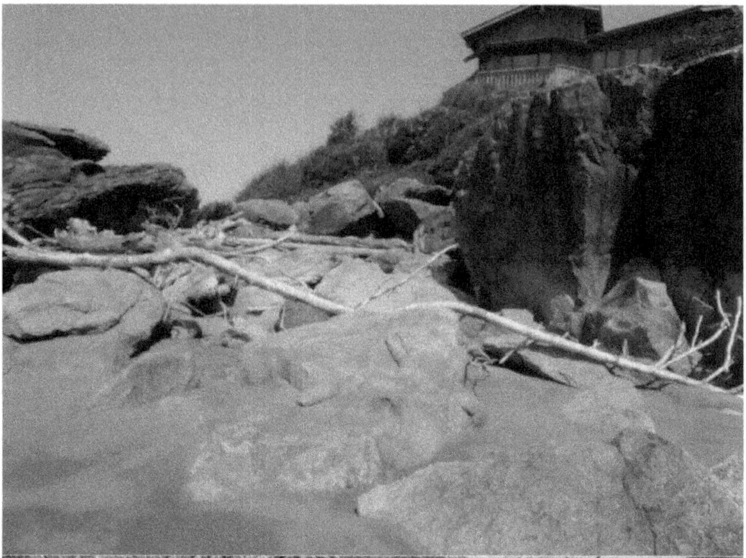

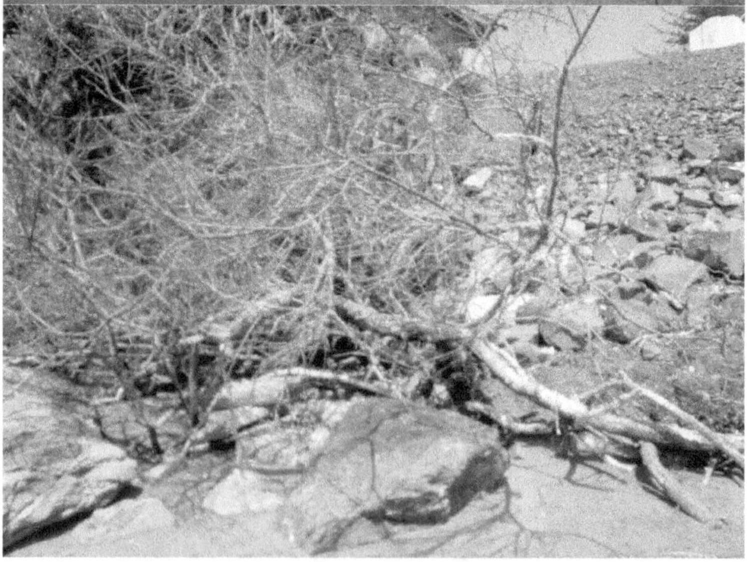

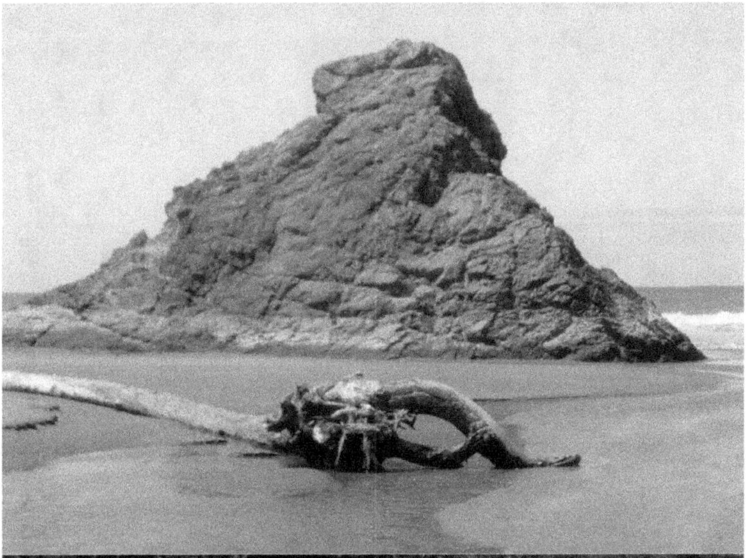

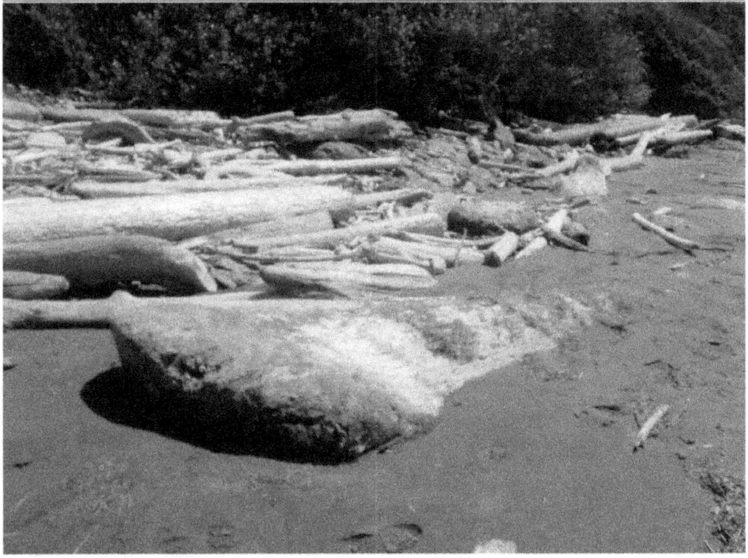

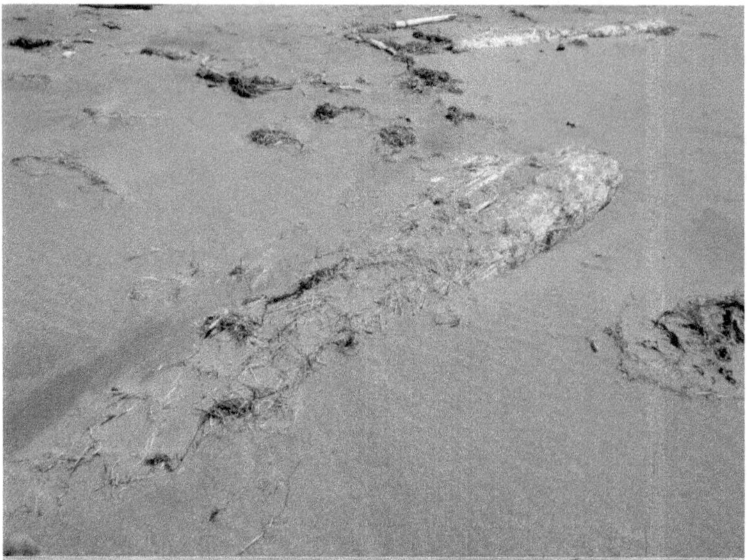
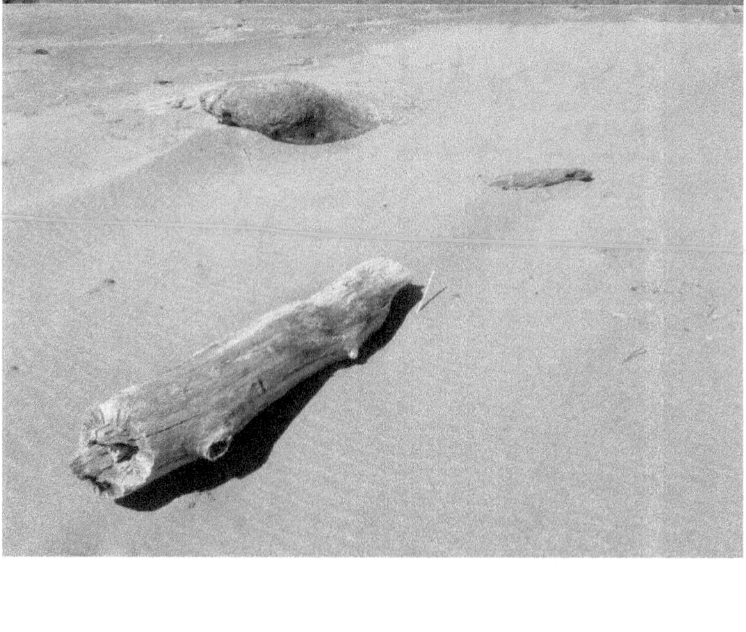

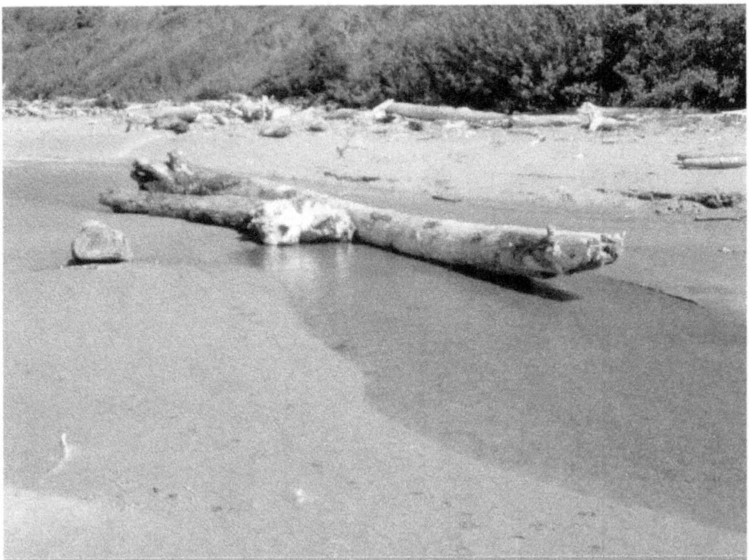

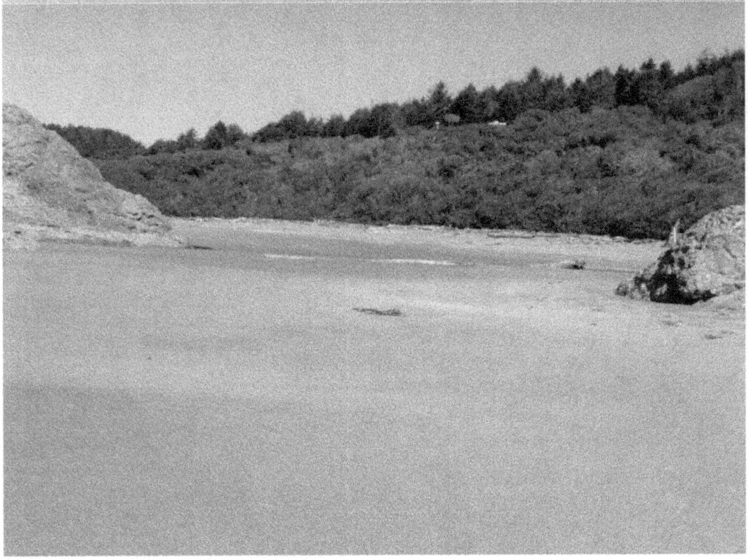

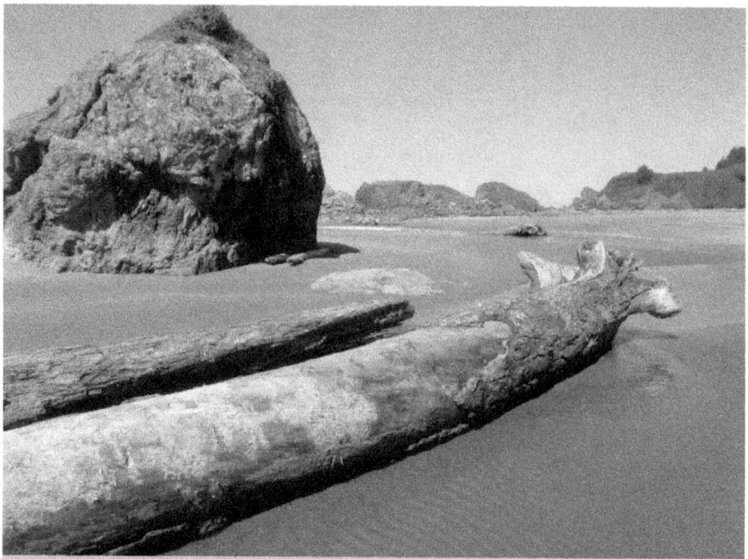

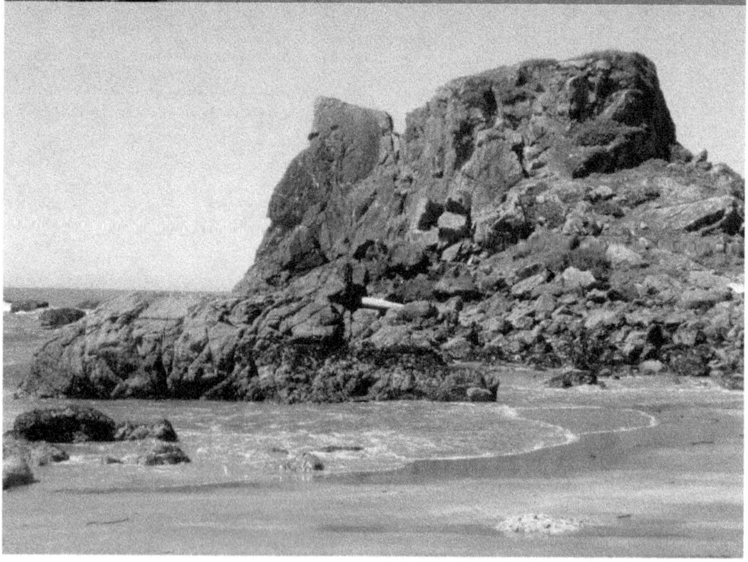

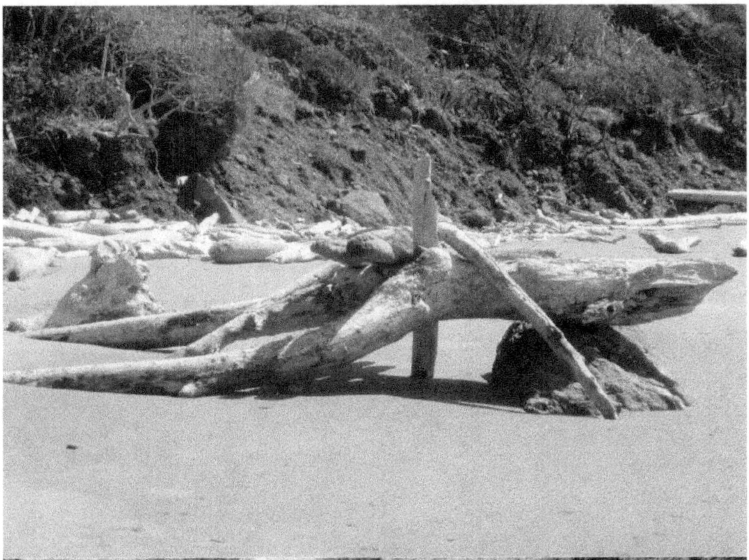

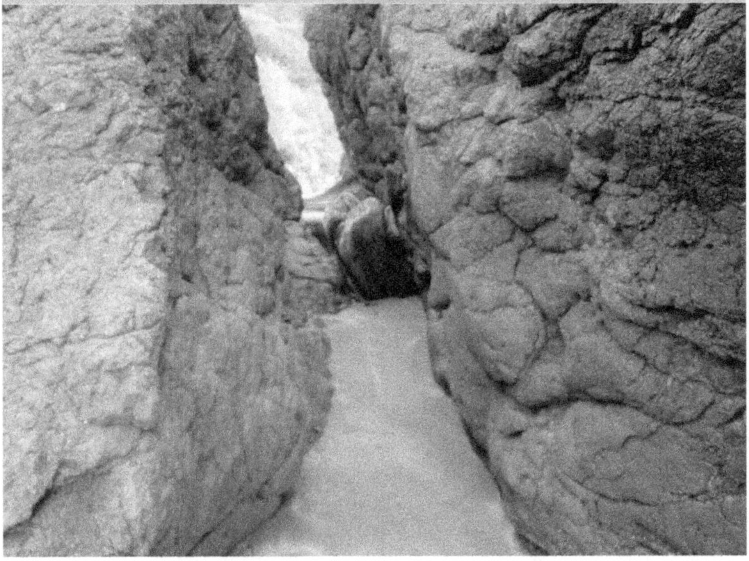

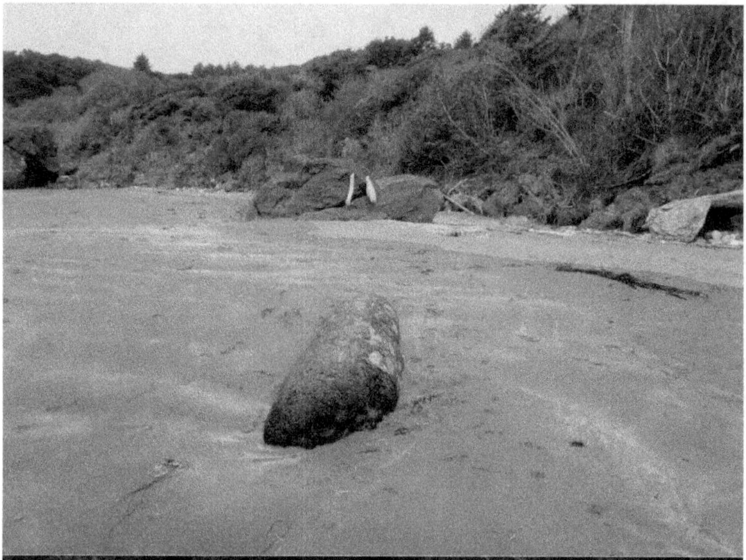

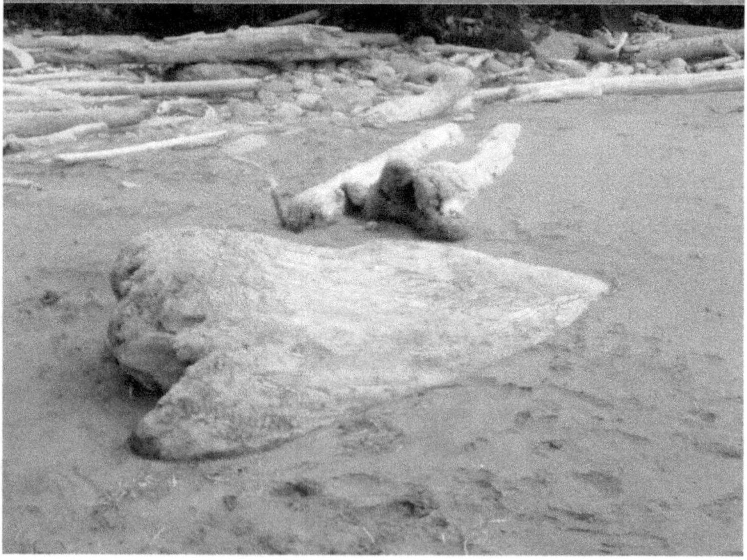

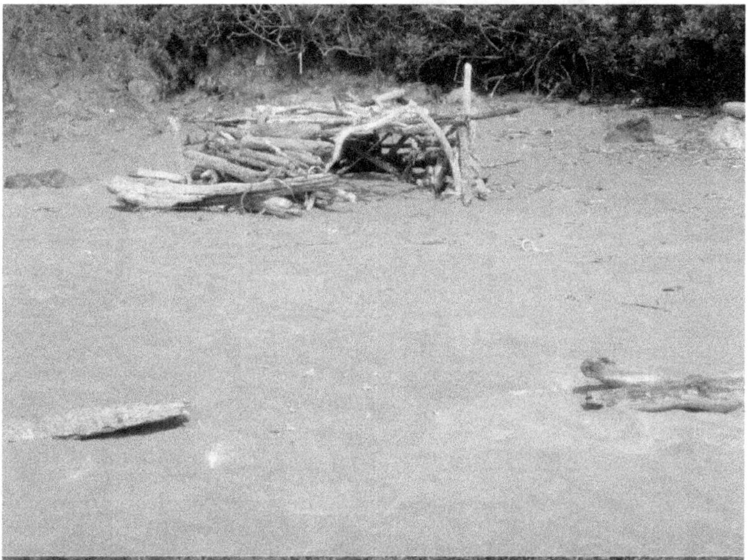
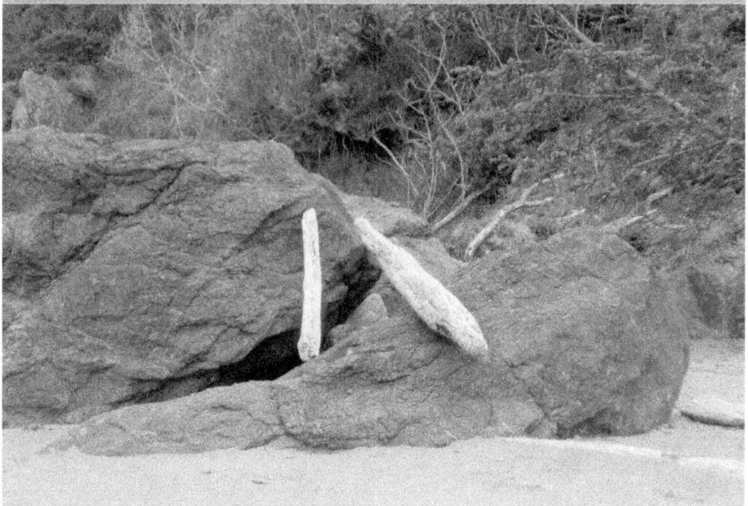

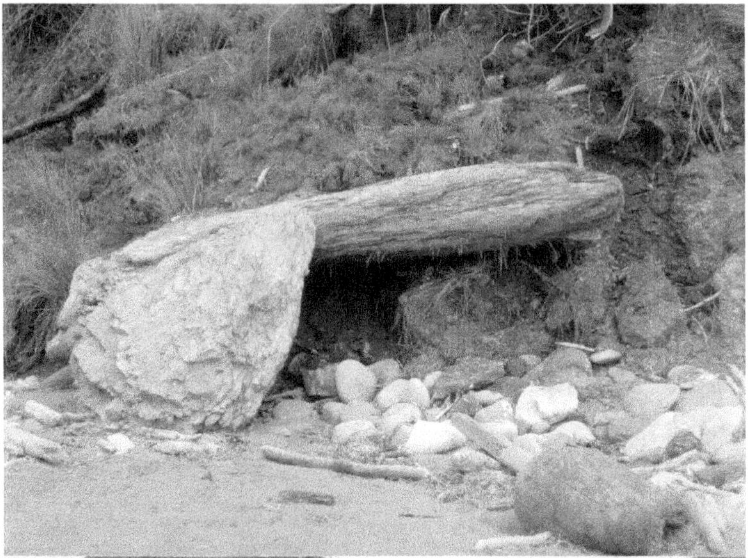

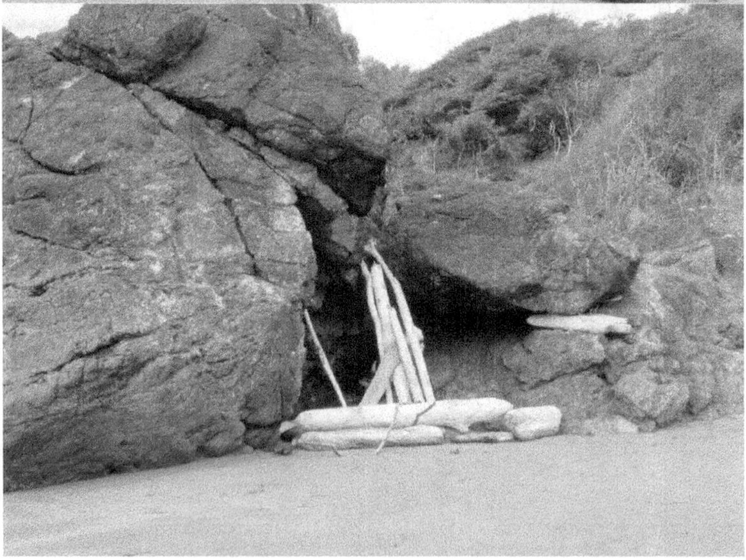

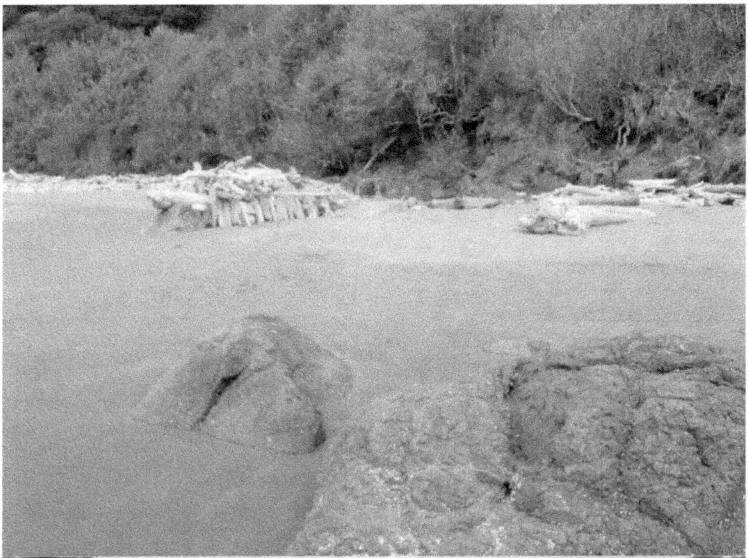
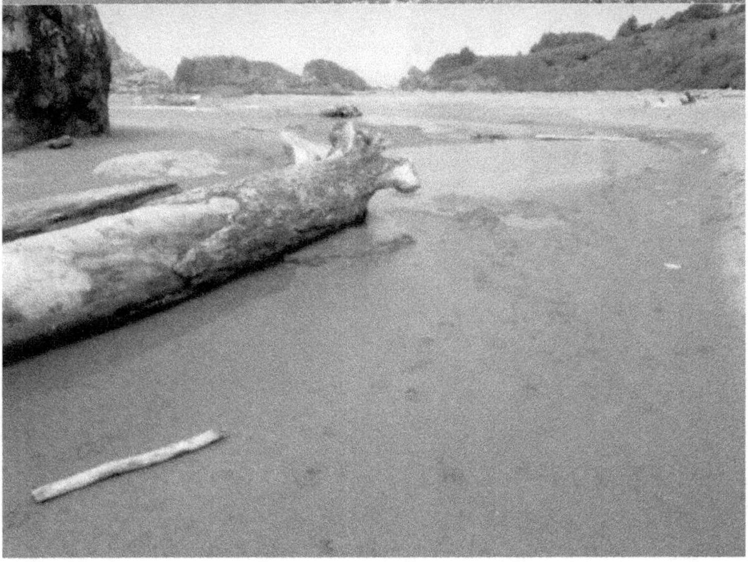

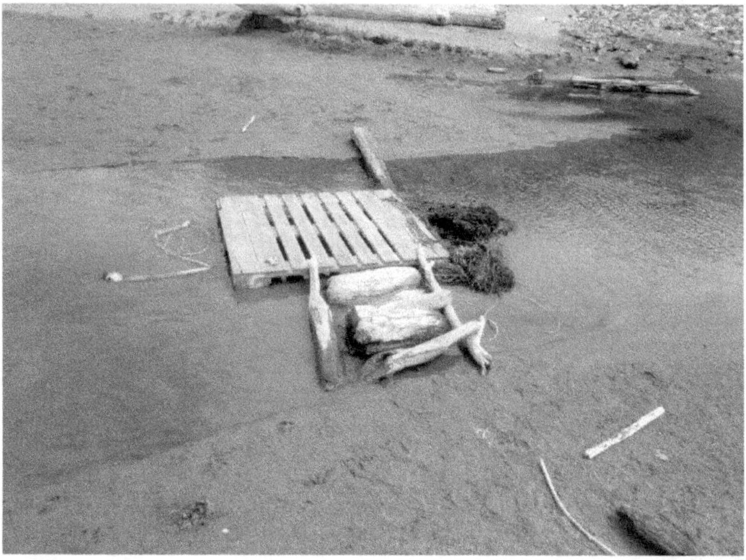

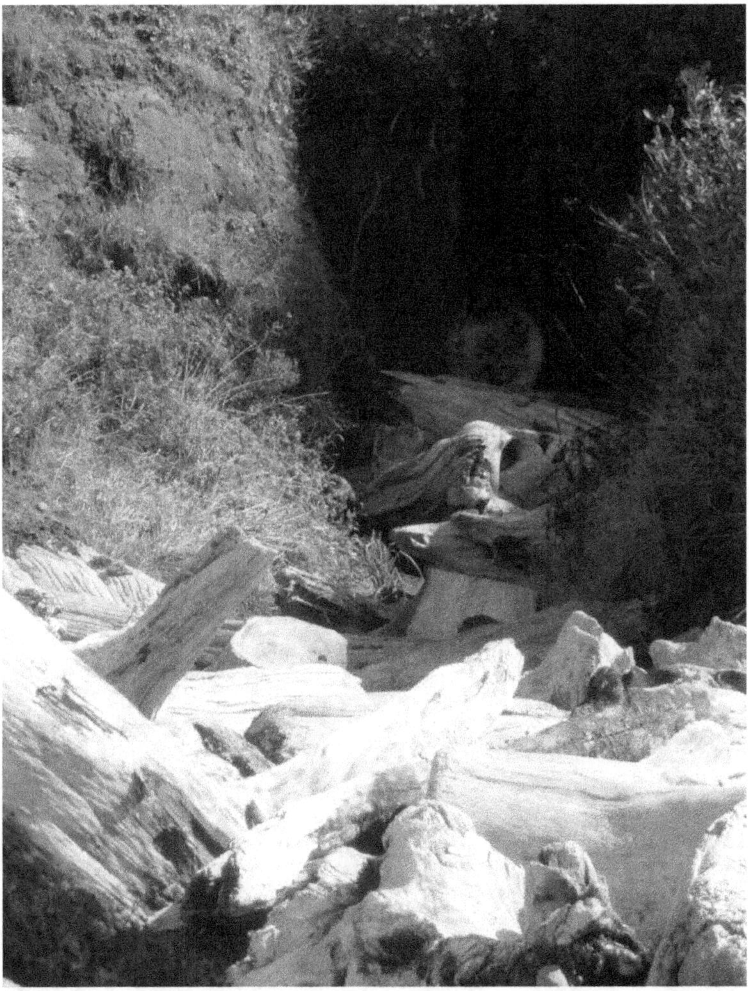

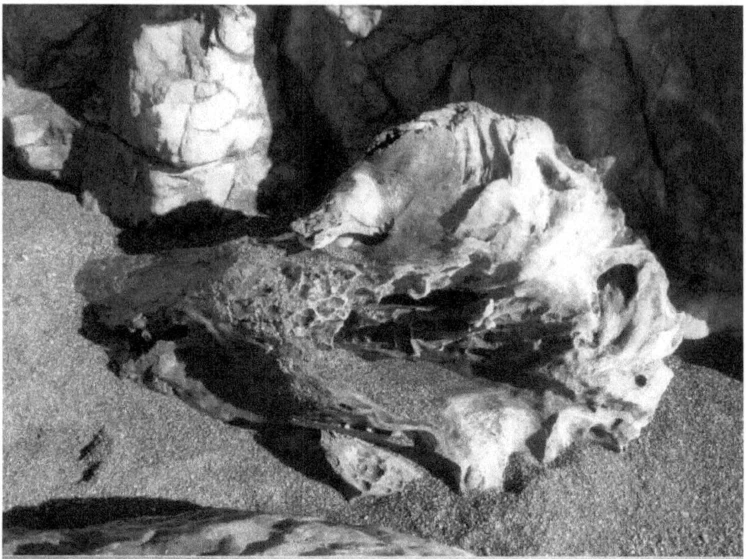

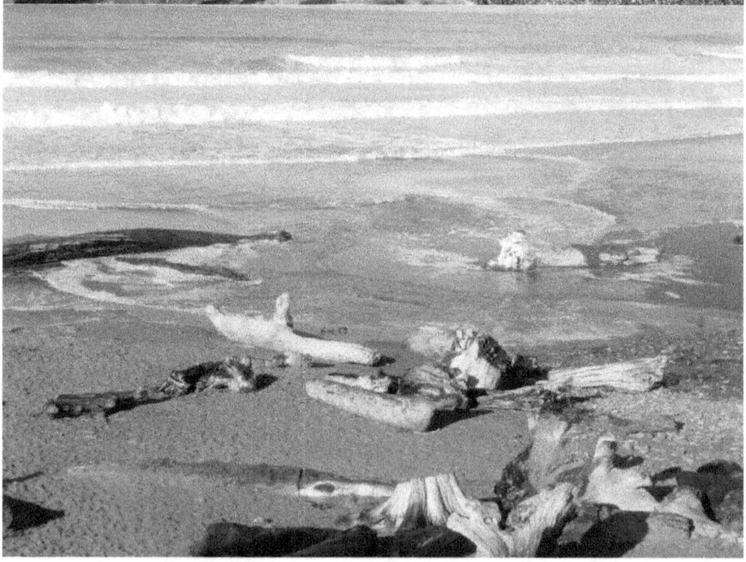

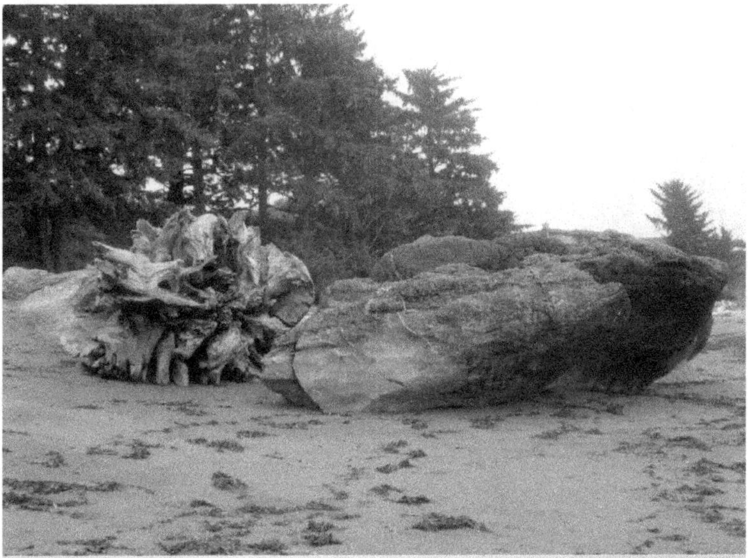

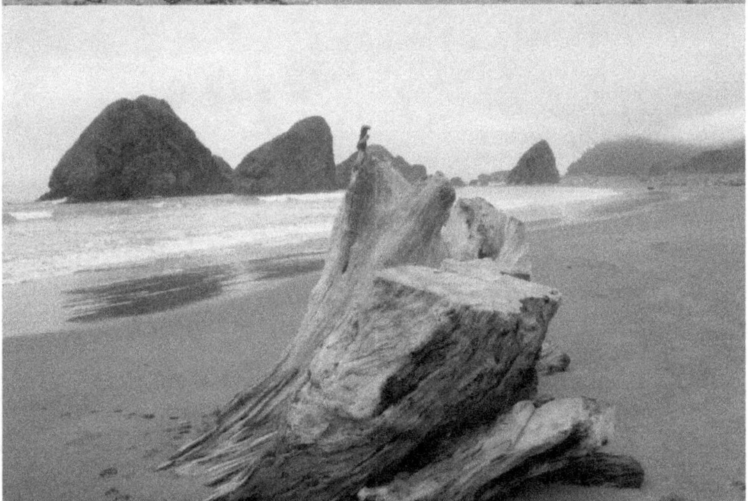

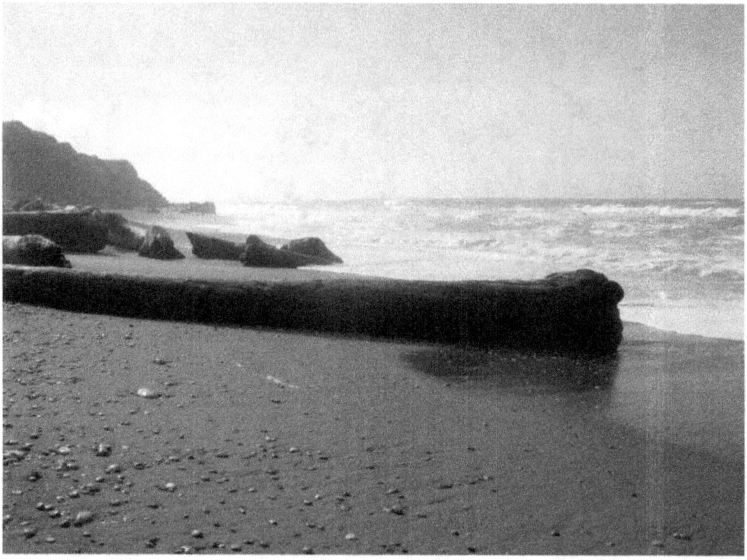

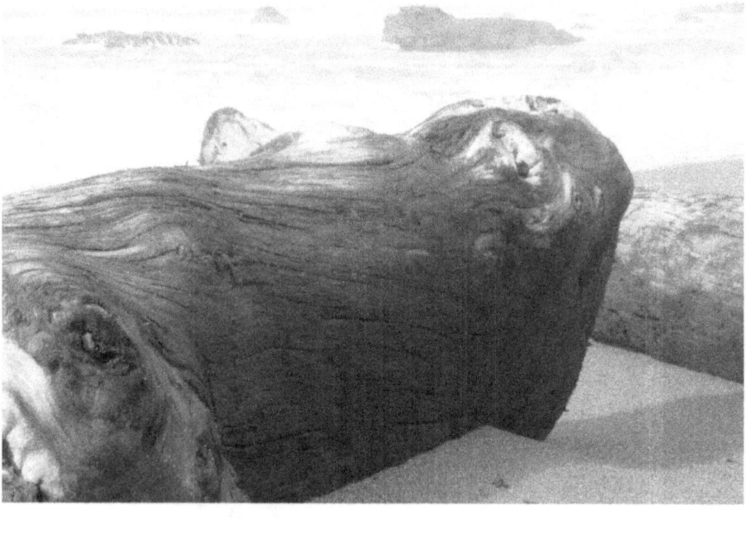

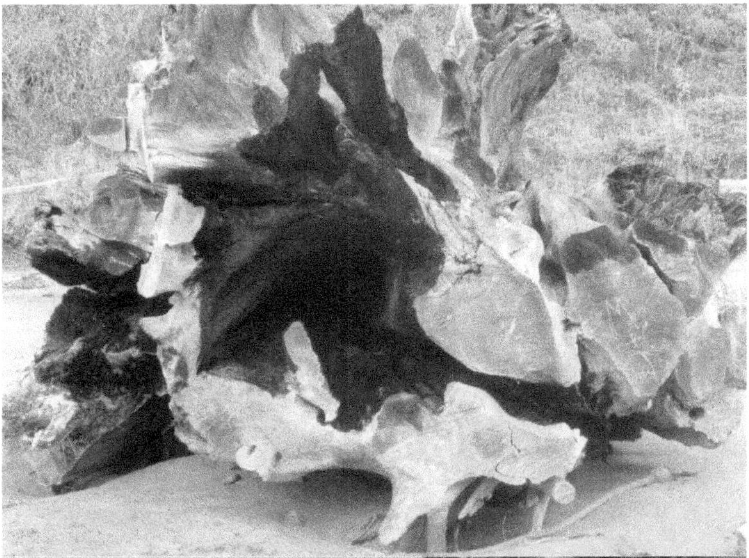

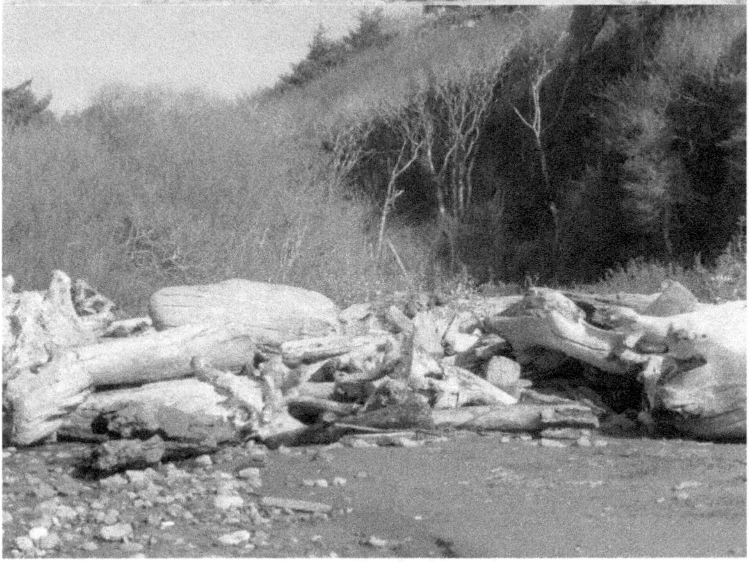

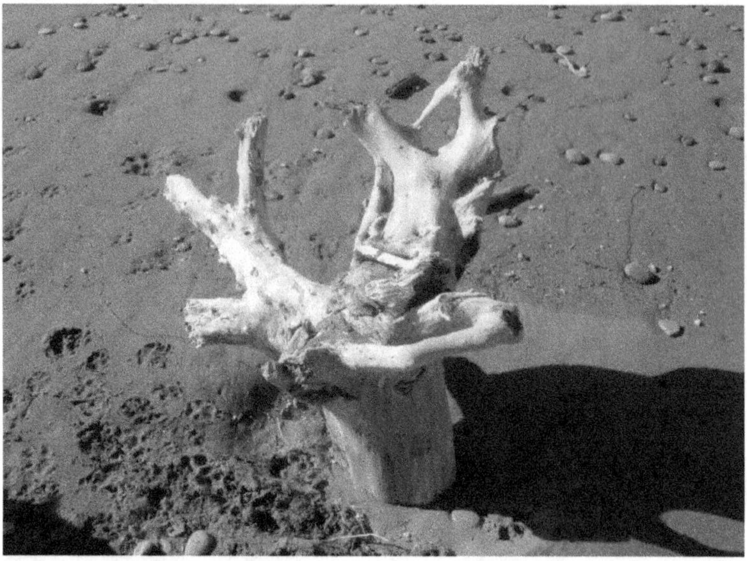

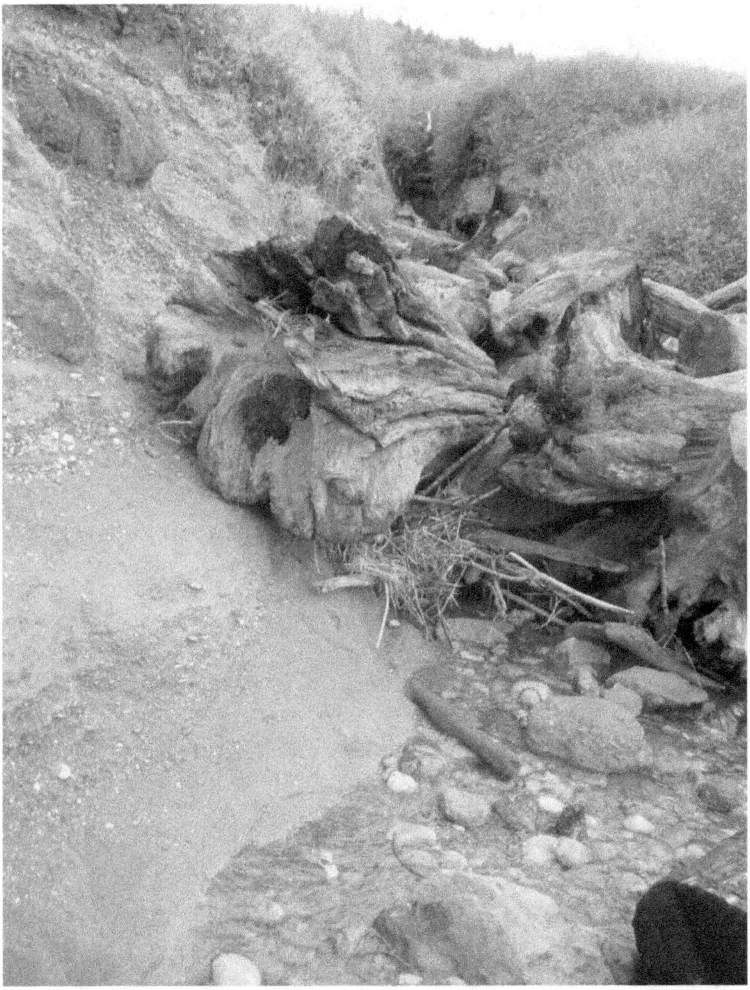

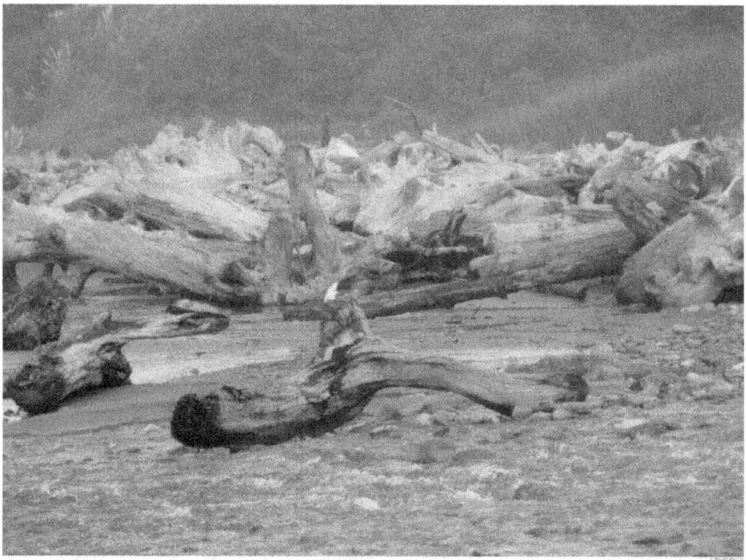

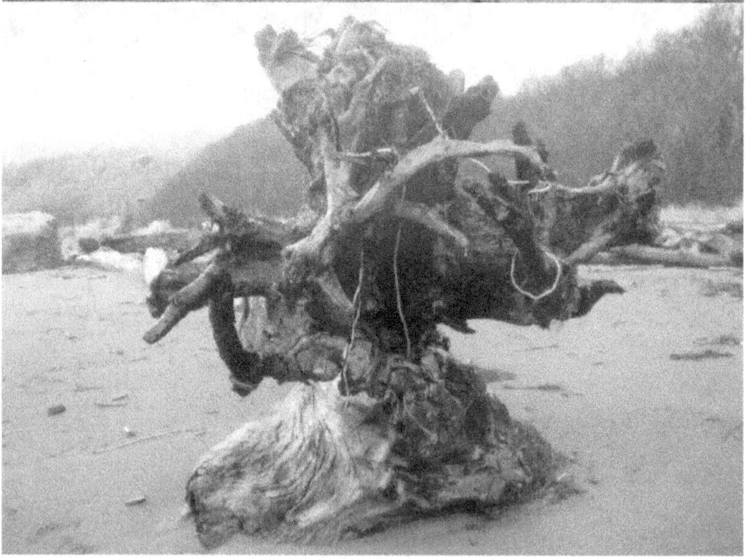

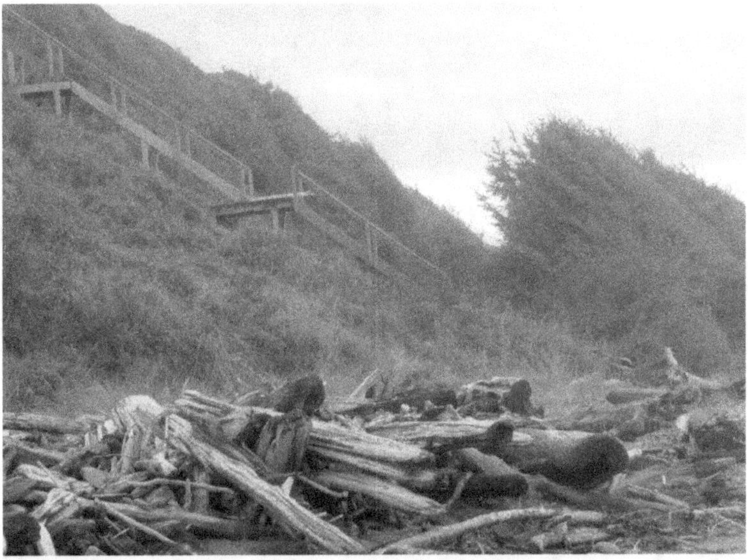

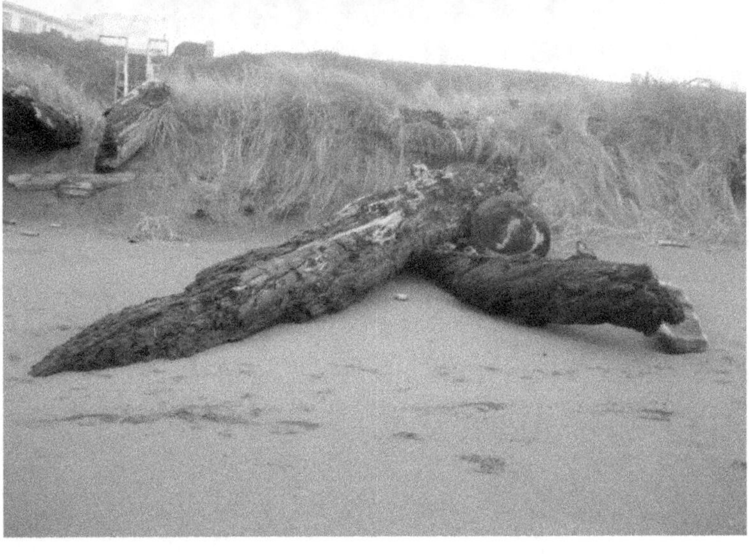

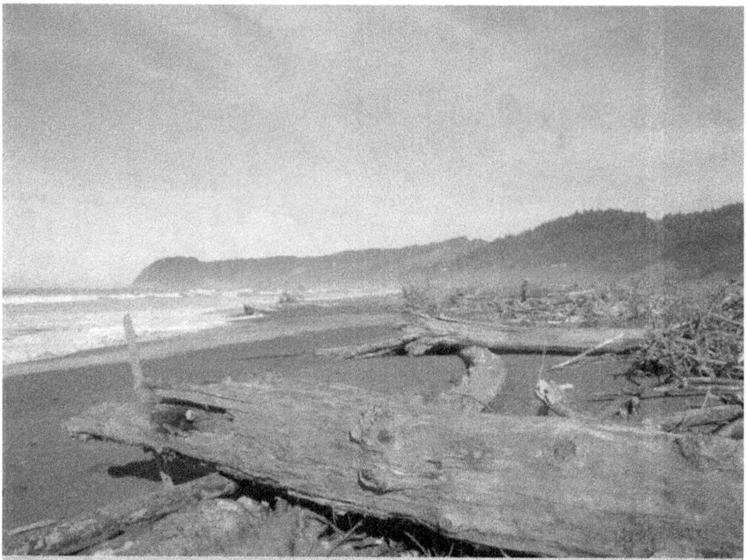

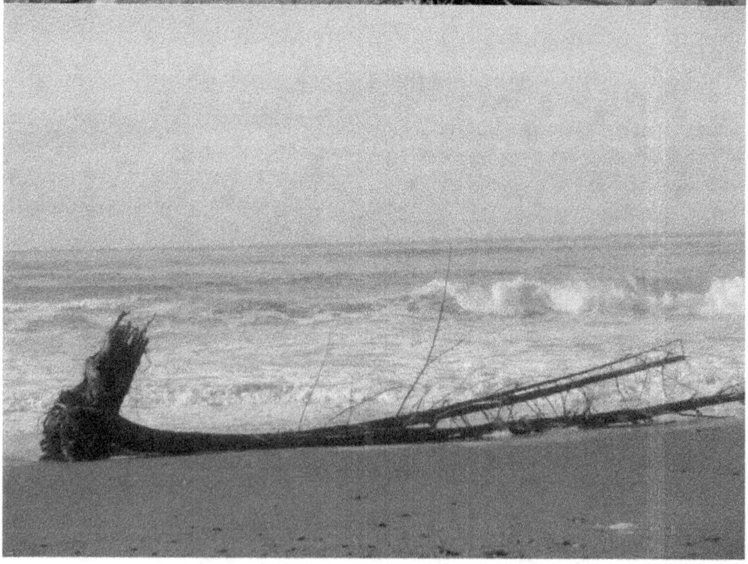

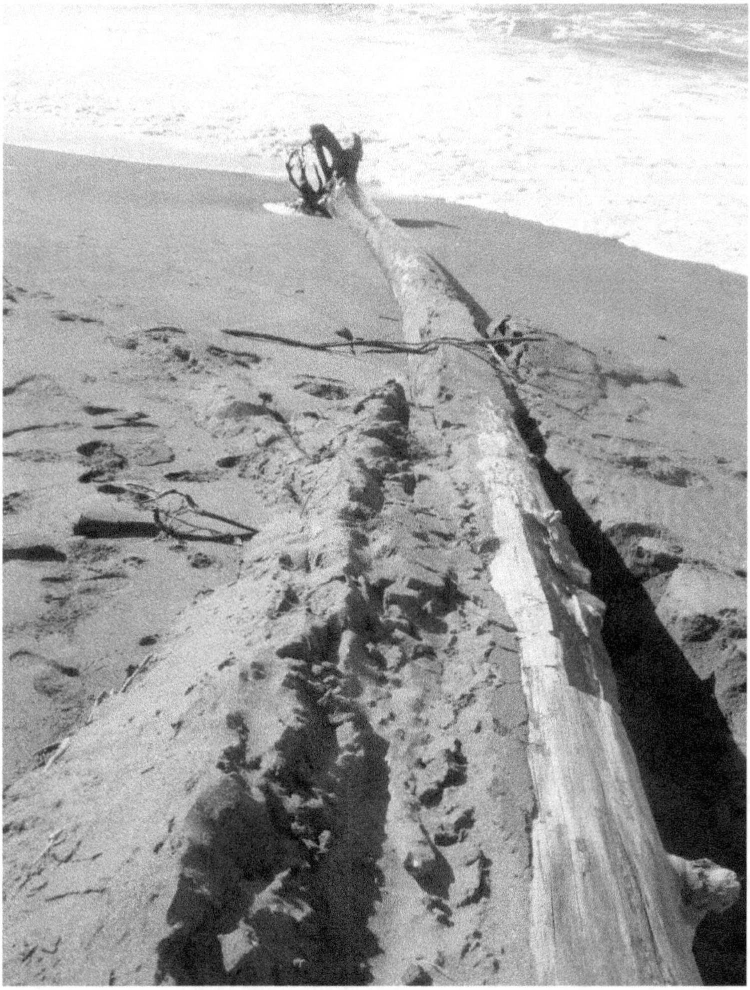

THE END

www.ingramcontent.com/pod-product-compliance
Lightning Source LLC
Chambersburg PA
CBHW070747180526
45168CB00004B/1556